The Universal Desires

Crafting Wealth through Human Nature

Introduction: The Nature of Desire

A brief philosophical and psychological discussion on human desires and their role as driving forces for progress and accumulation of wealth.

Human Desires: Catalysts for Progress and Wealth Accumulation

Human desires have been pivotal in shaping the trajectory of civilization. These desires, ranging from the basic need for survival to the complex pursuit of self-actualization, serve as the engines of progress and the accumulation of wealth.

Philosophical and psychological perspectives offer valuable insights into how these internal drives influence human behavior and societal advancement.

The Nature of Human Desires

From a philosophical standpoint, desires have been scrutinized since antiquity. Plato categorized desires into three types: the appetitive (bodily desires), the spirited (desires for honor and recognition), and the rational (intellectual aspirations). These categories highlight the multifaceted nature of human drives and their capacity to propel individuals toward growth or stagnation, depending on how they are managed.

In psychology, Abraham Maslow's hierarchy of needs provides a framework for understanding the stages of human motivation. At the foundation lie physiological and safety needs, followed by social belonging, esteem, and self-actualization. Maslow posited that unmet desires at any level could inhibit progress, but their fulfillment often leads to higher aspirations and greater achievements.

Desires as Engines of Progress

Desires for innovation, discovery, and betterment have historically driven progress. The pursuit of knowledge, for instance, has led to transformative advancements in science, technology, and the arts. This progress often begins with dissatisfaction—a fundamental psychological response that spurs individuals to seek improvement.

Adam Smith's concept of the "invisible hand" in economics underscores the idea that individual desires for wealth and personal gain can inadvertently benefit society as a whole. Entrepreneurs driven by profit motives innovate to meet consumer needs, thereby creating jobs and fostering economic growth.

The Paradox of Accumulation

While desires fuel progress, they also give rise to ethical and psychological dilemmas. The accumulation of wealth, often seen as a measure of success, can lead to both fulfillment and emptiness. Philosophers such as Epicurus warned against excessive desires, advocating for a life of moderation to achieve true happiness. Similarly, contemporary psychology identifies the "hedonic treadmill," where the pursuit of ever-greater wealth or pleasure results in diminishing returns on happiness.

However, accumulation also has a positive side. Wealth enables individuals and societies to invest in education, healthcare, and infrastructure, thus laying the groundwork for sustained progress. The challenge lies in balancing the pursuit of wealth with ethical considerations and emotional well-being.

The Societal Implications

At a societal level, collective desires manifest in cultural and economic trends. The Renaissance, for example, was fueled by a collective yearning for knowledge and artistic expression, leading to unparalleled achievements in human history. Conversely, unchecked desires can lead to social inequality, environmental degradation, and conflict.

Modern societies must grapple with how to harness desires for the greater good. Policies that encourage sustainable innovation, equitable wealth distribution, and ethical consumption can help channel human drives in constructive directions.

To sum up this brief introduction, human desires are both a blessing and a challenge. They are the driving forces behind progress and the accumulation of wealth, yet they also pose risks when left unchecked. Philosophical and psychological insights remind us that understanding and managing these desires is crucial for personal fulfillment and societal well-being. By striking a balance between ambition and moderation, humanity can continue to thrive while addressing the complexities of its inner drives.

Chapter 1: Power and Authority

The Male Pursuit of Strength

Understanding Strength, Leadership, and Dominance:

The male pursuit of strength has been a defining feature of human behavior throughout history. Strength, whether physical, intellectual, or social, has often been linked to leadership and dominance, shaping societal hierarchies and power structures. This interplay is evident in various domains, from the political arena to the corporate world, where influential figures leverage their authority to achieve remarkable feats.

Real-World Examples:

Business Tycoons: Figures like Elon Musk and Jeff Bezos exemplify how strength in vision, risk-taking, and resilience can lead to dominance in the business world. Their ability to influence markets, set trends, and inspire innovation underscores the role of leadership in accumulating wealth and influence.

Politicians: Leaders such as Winston Churchill and Nelson Mandela demonstrate how strength in oratory, strategy, and decision-making can mobilize nations and change the course of history. Their dominance in political landscapes reflects their capacity to inspire loyalty and shape collective futures.

Historical Figures: Historical icons like Alexander the Great and Genghis Khan illustrate the raw application of strength and dominance in achieving expansive empires. Their leadership not only secured their legacies but also altered global trajectories.

Strategies to Harness Leadership Skills and Build Authority:

Develop Self-Awareness: Understanding one's strengths and weaknesses is crucial for authentic leadership. Regular reflection and feedback can help refine one's approach to authority.

Cultivate Communication Skills: Persuasive communication is a hallmark of influential leaders. Mastering the art of storytelling and active listening can significantly enhance one's ability to lead.

Foster Emotional Intelligence: Empathy and emotional regulation are critical for building trust and motivating teams. Leaders who exhibit emotional intelligence tend to foster stronger, more cohesive groups.

Set a Vision and Inspire Action: Effective leaders articulate clear goals and inspire others to work towards them. Sharing a compelling vision can align efforts and amplify collective strength.

Build Resilience and Adaptability: The ability to navigate challenges and adapt to changing circumstances is essential for maintaining authority and achieving long-term success.

Conclusion

The pursuit of strength, leadership, and dominance is a powerful motivator that has shaped human behavior and societal development. By studying the strategies and traits of successful figures, individuals can learn to harness their own potential for leadership and build authority in their chosen fields. Balancing ambition with empathy and vision can lead to not only personal success but also meaningful contributions to society.

The next section will highlight Leveraging the desire for power by marketing products that symbolize authority and dominance, such as luxury cars, high-end watches, executive training courses, and leadership tools. Highlight exclusivity, success stories, and elite branding to push consumption.

The Male Pursuit of Strength: Selling Insights

The desire for power and dominance is a potent motivator that can be strategically leveraged in marketing. Products that symbolize authority and success, such as luxury cars, high-end watches, executive training courses, and leadership tools, naturally appeal to individuals seeking to assert their dominance and enhance their status. By emphasizing exclusivity, success stories, and elite branding, marketers can create a compelling narrative that drives consumption.

Key Strategies to Market Products That Symbolize Power

Emphasize Exclusivity:

Position products as rare and accessible only to a select few. Luxury brands like Rolex and Rolls-Royce excel at crafting an aura of exclusivity, making ownership a status symbol.

Use limited-edition releases, VIP memberships, or personalized services to heighten the sense of privilege.

Highlight Success Stories:

Showcase testimonials from influential figures or high-achievers who use the product. Real-world examples can inspire aspirational buyers to associate the product with their desired status.

Create case studies or video campaigns featuring individuals who achieved remarkable success through the product, such as graduates of executive training programs or users of cutting-edge leadership tools.

Leverage Elite Branding:

Develop branding that exudes sophistication, power, and prestige. Use bold typography, sleek designs, and premium materials to reflect the authority associated with the product.

Partner with luxury events, high-profile influencers, or exclusive clubs to strengthen the association with power and dominance.

Create a Narrative of Empowerment:

Market products as tools that empower individuals to take control and lead. For example, a high-end watch can symbolize a person's mastery of time and success in achieving goals.

Use slogans or campaigns that inspire confidence, such as "Own the Moment" or "Command Your Destiny."

Incorporate Visuals That Symbolize Authority:

Use imagery of powerful leaders, high-performing individuals, and iconic symbols of success. Include visuals of boardrooms, luxury offices, or influential settings to appeal to ambition-driven consumers.

Examples of Power-Centric Products and Campaigns

Luxury Cars:

Brands like Ferrari and Bentley market their vehicles not just as modes of transportation but as statements of power and prestige. Ad campaigns often emphasize the craftsmanship, exclusivity, and association with influential personalities.

High-End Watches:

Timepieces from brands like Patek Philippe and Omega are marketed as symbols of legacy and authority. Their advertising frequently portrays successful, confident individuals in leadership roles.

Executive Training Courses:

Institutions like Harvard Business School promote their programs as gateways to elite networks and unparalleled opportunities, reinforcing the narrative of empowerment and leadership.

Leadership Tools:

Products like premium planners, decision-making software, or exclusive networking platforms can be marketed as indispensable assets for individuals aiming to rise to positions of authority.

The Psychological Appeal of Power Symbolism

Human psychology is deeply attuned to status and recognition. Owning or using products associated with power and dominance fulfills not only personal desires but also social validation. These products act as "badges of honor," signaling achievement and authority to peers.

In conclusion, marketing to the desire for power requires a nuanced understanding of human ambition and social dynamics. By positioning products as symbols of authority, dominance, and success, brands can tap into deep-seated aspirations and drive consumption. When executed effectively, such strategies not only elevate the product's perceived value but also create lasting brand loyalty among those who seek to lead and excel.

Next chapter, will discuss the impact of beauty and aesthetics in society, markets, and consumerism. How industries (e.g., fashion, cosmetics) thrive by catering to this desire. Practical insights: Identifying trends and opportunities in industries driven by aesthetics.

Chapter 2:

Beauty and Perception

– The Women's Pursuit of Aesthetics

The Influence of Aesthetics on Human Behavior

Beauty and aesthetics have always been integral to human experience. They affect how we perceive the world, influence personal and collective identities, and often serve as markers of status and culture. From the intricate sculptures of ancient Greece to the polished interfaces of modern technology, the pursuit of beauty has shaped innovations and industries alike.

Aesthetics are not merely superficial. Research in psychology shows that attractive designs and appearances trigger positive emotions, enhance perceived value, and influence decision-making. In markets, this translates into a powerful driver of consumerism, as individuals strive to associate themselves with objects, lifestyles, or brands that align with their aesthetic ideals.

Industries That Thrive on Aesthetic Appeal

Fashion and Luxury Goods:

The fashion industry is perhaps the most visible manifestation of society's obsession with beauty. High-end brands like Louis Vuitton and Prada thrive by offering products that signify exclusivity and artistry. Fast fashion giants like Zara and H&M tap into aesthetic trends at affordable price points, democratizing beauty while maintaining high turnover rates in styles.

Cosmetics and Skincare:

The global beauty industry, valued at hundreds of billions, is built on the promise of enhancement. From makeup that transforms appearances to skincare that claims to reverse aging, cosmetics cater to deep-seated desires for confidence and self-expression. Emerging trends, such as "clean beauty" and inclusive product lines, continue to drive growth by addressing evolving consumer priorities.

Home and Interior Design:

The aesthetic appeal of living spaces has become a significant market force. Furniture and decor companies like IKEA and West Elm cater to the desire for visually appealing homes, while bespoke interior design services offer personalized beauty. Movements like minimalism or maximalism demonstrate how aesthetic trends influence consumer preferences.

Tech and Industrial Design:

Companies like Apple have demonstrated that aesthetics and functionality can coexist to create iconic products. The appeal of sleek, intuitive, and visually appealing designs elevates consumer perception, positioning such products as status symbols.

Identifying Trends and Opportunities in Aesthetic-Driven Industries

Sustainability and Aesthetics:

As consumers prioritize environmental responsibility, industries that combine beauty with eco-friendly practices are gaining traction. Brands like Stella McCartney and Fenty Beauty have shown that sustainability and aesthetics can go hand-in-hand. Opportunities lie in innovative packaging, materials, and processes that reduce environmental impact without compromising visual appeal.

Customization and Personalization:

Today consumers increasingly value products that reflect their individuality. Services offering customizable fashion, bespoke beauty formulations, or personalized interior design solutions present significant opportunities to cater to unique tastes and preferences.

Diverse and Inclusive Standards:

The global market is shifting toward broader definitions of beauty. Industries that celebrate diverse identities, body types, and cultures are finding new audiences and building stronger consumer loyalty. Examples include cosmetics brands offering extensive shade ranges or clothing lines designed for various body shapes.

Digital Platforms and Aesthetic Marketing:

The visual nature of social media platforms like Instagram and Pinterest has amplified the importance of aesthetics in marketing. Businesses that invest in high-quality imagery, influencer collaborations, and immersive digital experiences gain a competitive edge. Virtual try-ons and augmented reality (AR) tools also enhance engagement by blending beauty with technology.

Practical Insights for Entrepreneurs and Businesses

Monitor Emerging Trends: Stay ahead by observing global trends in beauty and aesthetics, including cultural shifts, technological advances, and changing consumer values.

- *Invest in Storytelling:* Effective branding combines aesthetics with compelling narratives that resonate emotionally with consumers.
- *Collaborate with Influencers:* Partnering with creators who align with your brand's aesthetic helps amplify reach and authenticity.
- *Focus on Quality and Experience:* Consumers drawn to beauty often value not just the product but the experience of ownership and interaction.

Conclusion

The desire for beauty and aesthetic appeal is deeply embedded in human nature, making it a powerful force in shaping society and markets. Industries that cater to these desires thrive by tapping into aspirations, emotions, and identity. By understanding the evolving dynamics of aesthetic-driven consumerism and adapting to emerging trends, businesses can unlock significant growth opportunities and establish lasting connections with their audiences.

Next section will discuss examples of how to capitalize on the beauty industry by offering cosmetics, fashion, skincare, and fitness products that promise transformation and self-confidence. Use aspirational marketing, influencers, and visuals to appeal to the pursuit of perfection and aesthetics.

Beauty and Perception – The Women's Pursuit of Aesthetics - Selling Insights

Examples of Capitalizing on the Beauty Industry

Cosmetics:

- ✓ Offer transformative products like contour kits, highlighters, or bold lipsticks that promise instant changes in appearance.

- ✓ Use aspirational marketing that showcases "before and after" transformations, emphasizing self-confidence and allure.

✓ Collaborate with influencers who embody aspirational beauty to showcase tutorials and testimonials, building trust and desire for the product.

Fashion:

- Design collections that align with current trends while offering customization options to appeal to individuality.

- Create high-impact visual campaigns featuring aspirational figures, emphasizing themes like empowerment, sophistication, or freedom.

- Leverage limited-edition drops to create exclusivity and urgency, driving demand.

Skincare:

- Promote products with "science-backed" claims to target issues like aging, acne, or dullness, offering solutions that seem credible and transformative.

- Invest in social media campaigns with aesthetically pleasing content, including glowing skin transformations and minimalist product displays.

- Partner with dermatologists and wellness influencers to endorse the product's effectiveness.

Fitness Products:

- Market fitness apparel, equipment, or supplements as essential tools for achieving an "ideal" body.

- Use aspirational imagery, such as toned athletes or influencers performing workouts in stylish gear, to create an emotional connection.

- Offer programs that pair products with "lifestyle" benefits, like access to exclusive workout plans or virtual training sessions.

- Identifying Trends and Opportunities in Aesthetic-Driven Industries

Sustainability and Ethical Practices:

Eco-conscious consumers are increasingly drawn to brands that merge aesthetics with sustainable practices. Opportunities lie in creating products that are both beautiful and environmentally friendly.

Personalization:

Customization is a growing trend, allowing consumers to tailor products to their unique tastes and preferences. Fashion and cosmetics brands offering personalized services have a competitive edge.

Digital Presence and Aesthetic Marketing:

The rise of social media has amplified the importance of visual branding. Industries that invest in high-quality imagery, influencer partnerships, and immersive digital experiences stand out in a crowded marketplace.

Inclusivity in Beauty Standards:

Expanding definitions of beauty to embrace diverse cultures, body types, and identities presents opportunities for brands to connect with broader audiences.

Practical Insights for Entrepreneurs and Businesses

Monitor Emerging Trends: Stay ahead by observing global trends in beauty and aesthetics, including cultural shifts, technological advances, and changing consumer values.

Invest in Storytelling: Effective branding combines aesthetics with compelling narratives that resonate emotionally with consumers.

Collaborate with Influencers: Partnering with creators who align with your brand's aesthetic helps amplify reach and authenticity.

Focus on Quality and Experience: Consumers drawn to beauty often value not just the product but the experience of ownership and interaction.

Conclusion

Beauty and aesthetics are powerful forces that influence consumer behavior, societal values, and market dynamics. Industries that cater to these desires not only thrive economically but also shape cultural narratives. By identifying and adapting to emerging trends, businesses can innovate and create products that resonate deeply with aesthetic-driven consumers, ensuring long-term success.

Next chapter will explore the global wellness and healthcare economy. How businesses innovate to meet the growing needs of an aging population. Then will give some practical insights like Investing in and creating solutions that enhance quality of life.

Chapter 3: Longevity and Health – The Elderly's Desire for Wellness

The Global Wellness and Healthcare Economy

Innovations for an Aging Population

As populations around the world grow older, the wellness and healthcare economy is undergoing significant transformation. Businesses are rising to meet the challenges and opportunities presented by an aging demographic, driving innovation in products, services, and technology.

Healthcare Technology:

Telemedicine platforms, wearable health devices, and AI-driven diagnostics are reshaping how healthcare is delivered. Companies like Philips and Medtronic are at the forefront, providing solutions that prioritize accessibility and efficiency.

Senior Living and Assisted Care:

The demand for senior-friendly living spaces has spurred growth in assisted living facilities, home care services, and smart home technologies designed to enhance independence and safety.

Pharmaceutical and Biotech Advancements:

Research into age-related diseases, such as Alzheimer's and arthritis, has led to breakthroughs in treatments and therapies. Innovations in personalized medicine are tailoring care to individual genetic profiles, improving outcomes for older patients.

Wellness Products and Services:

Beyond medical care, the wellness industry caters to aging populations through fitness programs, nutrition plans, and mental health resources that promote holistic well-being.

Financial Services for Aging Populations:

Retirement planning tools, insurance products, and financial literacy programs are being developed to address the specific needs of seniors, ensuring long-term security and peace of mind.

Opportunities for Businesses

Adapting Products for Accessibility:

Companies can modify existing products to suit aging consumers, such as creating ergonomic designs or developing apps with simplified interfaces.

Focusing on Preventative Care:

Businesses that emphasize health maintenance through fitness, diet, and wellness coaching can capture a growing market of proactive seniors.

Community Building:

Establishing networks or platforms that foster social engagement among older adults helps combat isolation and builds brand loyalty.

Leveraging Data and AI:

Using data analytics to predict trends and customize offerings allows businesses to stay ahead of the curve in meeting the needs of aging consumers.

Conclusion

The global wellness and healthcare economy is uniquely positioned to address the challenges of an aging population while unlocking vast economic potential. By prioritizing innovation and empathy, businesses can not only meet the needs of older demographics but also build lasting value and trust in an evolving marketplace.

The next chapter discuss the multi-billion-dollar entertainment, gaming, and education sectors. How brands capture children's attention and convert play into profit. Practical insights: Building products and platforms that inspire and entertain youth.

Chapter 4:

Play and Imagination

– The Children's World of Games

The multi-billion-dollar entertainment, gaming, and education sectors have increasingly become interconnected, with brands developing strategies that not only capture children's attention but also turn their play and engagement into profit. To succeed in these sectors, companies must create products and platforms that blend entertainment, learning, and interaction in ways that resonate with young audiences. Here are some practical insights into how brands achieve this:

1. Gamification in Education

Brands in the education sector are tapping into the powerful concept of gamification—integrating game-like elements into educational tools to make learning engaging and fun.

Example: Duolingo

Duolingo, a language-learning app, uses elements of gaming such as points, levels, and achievements to motivate users. The app makes learning a new language feel like a game, using friendly characters and fun challenges that children enjoy.

Insight:

By combining education and entertainment, brands like Duolingo maintain engagement and inspire kids to keep coming back for more. Using rewards, progress tracking, and game mechanics such as leaderboards, brands ensure that children see learning as a form of play.

2. Interactive and Personalized Gaming Experiences

The gaming industry is evolving to create deeply personalized, interactive experiences that keep children immersed. Developers use data analytics and AI to adapt content to individual players' interests and behaviors.

Example: Roblox

Roblox allows players to create their own games within the platform. This "user-generated content" approach not only fosters creativity but also enables kids to monetize their creations through in-game purchases and selling virtual items. This platform has become a social space where play and creativity intersect with real-world value.

Insight:

Children today crave autonomy and the ability to influence their environment. Brands that allow for creativity and personalization, like Roblox, can captivate children's attention and build a community that supports profit generation through microtransactions.

3. Influencer Marketing and Brand Ambassadors

Brands in these sectors often turn to child influencers or characters that resonate with young audiences. This strategy capitalizes on the influence of popular figures within the gaming, educational, or entertainment realms to boost brand loyalty and increase sales.

Example: YouTube Kids & Gaming Influencers

Platforms like YouTube Kids feature popular gaming influencers who play games and provide entertaining commentary. These influencers often partner with brands, leading children to engage with games, products, and services promoted by these personalities.

Insight:

Children tend to trust their favorite YouTube stars or characters more than traditional advertisements. By associating with influencers or embedding characters that kids already love, brands can create authentic connections that lead to conversion and ongoing loyalty.

4. Subscription Models and Microtransactions

Subscription-based models (such as Netflix for kids or educational apps) and microtransactions in games allow brands to sustain revenue streams while offering ongoing value to children. This model keeps kids engaged with exclusive content or features, and parents are often willing to pay for content that educates or entertains their children.

Example: Disney+ and Netflix

Disney+ and Netflix cater specifically to children's content with age-appropriate shows, movies, and even interactive content (e.g., "Bandersnatch" on Netflix). These platforms ensure kids stay engaged by continually releasing fresh content that sparks excitement.

Insight:

Subscriptions and in-app purchases are lucrative because they turn one-time interactions into repeat business. By offering exclusive, fresh content and interactive features, platforms can increase retention and create predictable revenue.

5. Augmented Reality (AR) and Virtual Reality (VR)

The use of AR and VR in children's entertainment is gaining momentum, offering immersive experiences that blend the digital and physical worlds. These technologies have the potential to elevate gaming and educational platforms into something far more engaging and memorable.

Example: Pokémon GO

Pokémon GO is one of the most successful examples of AR gaming. Players use their mobile devices to hunt virtual Pokémon in the real world, combining physical movement with a digital game. This game had a massive impact on children and families, encouraging them to explore and be active while engaging with the beloved franchise.

Insight:

By creating experiences that combine the real and digital worlds, brands can encourage children to spend more time with their products while promoting physical activity or social interaction. AR and VR offer endless potential for interactive storytelling, education, and gaming.

6. Cross-Platform Engagement

Children today engage with brands across multiple devices and platforms, and brands need to ensure that their products and content are accessible everywhere—on mobile apps, consoles, websites, and social media.

Example: Fortnite

Fortnite is not only a popular game, but also a social platform where players can engage in virtual events and concerts. The game has integrated live events, such as Travis Scott's virtual concert, to keep players engaged beyond the traditional gameplay. The game's cross-platform nature ensures that kids can play it on consoles, mobile phones, and PCs, keeping the game accessible and relevant.

Insight:

Children do not limit their interactions to one platform or device. Brands must ensure their products offer seamless cross-platform experiences to maintain relevance and keep children invested.

7. Incorporating Social Interaction and Communities

Children are highly social, and creating platforms or products that allow for social interaction among peers is key to building long-term engagement. Social features like chatting, multiplayer modes, or sharing content are all vital to keeping children hooked.

Example: Minecraft

Minecraft's multiplayer mode allows players to interact, build together, and share their creations. The game also offers a marketplace where players can purchase skins, textures, and other customizations. This combination of social interaction, creativity, and in-game purchases makes it a highly profitable platform.

Insight:

Social play drives engagement. Brands should prioritize creating features that allow kids to share their experiences, build communities, and interact with one another. This sense of connection keeps children coming back, creating a lasting relationship with the brand.

8. Child-Friendly Advertising and Privacy Compliance

Children are a highly protected demographic, with strict regulations on how brands can advertise to them. Brands in entertainment and education sectors are increasingly investing in child-friendly advertising models that comply with regulations like COPPA (Children's Online Privacy Protection Act).

Example: YouTube Kids' Parental Controls

YouTube Kids offers a safe environment where children can access age-appropriate content. It also provides parental control features, giving parents peace of mind while children engage with content. Additionally, YouTube Kids limits how ads are targeted and ensures that advertising content is suitable for children.

Insight:

Brands must comply with privacy laws and ensure their platforms provide safe, ethical advertising experiences. Transparency with parents about data usage and advertising practices is key to gaining trust.

Conclusion:

In order to succeed in the competitive and evolving entertainment, gaming, and education sectors, brands need to create engaging, interactive, and personalized experiences for children. By combining entertainment with learning, leveraging social features, offering cross-platform experiences, and adhering to privacy regulations, brands can turn play into profit while fostering a loyal and enthusiastic customer base. Ultimately, creating products that inspire creativity, social engagement, and joy ensures that kids keep coming back for more—and that parents are willing to support those choices.

Next chapter helps Understanding financial insecurities and poverty cycles. Strategies for creating value that addresses fears of loss and scarcity. Practical insights: Tackling solutions to empower underserved communities.

Chapter 5:

Fear of Scarcity

– Overcoming Poverty through Security

Understanding financial insecurities and poverty cycles is essential for creating effective solutions that can empower underserved communities. Financial insecurity and poverty often result from a combination of systemic barriers, limited access to resources, and a lack of economic opportunities. People in these communities are often trapped in cycles of scarcity, where fear of loss—whether of income, shelter, or basic needs—becomes a constant stressor. To address these issues, it's important to develop strategies that create sustainable value, reduce vulnerability, and empower individuals to break free from these cycles. Below are practical insights and strategies for tackling these problems and creating long-term solutions.

1. Building Financial Literacy and Empowerment

Financial literacy is a key factor in breaking the cycle of poverty. People who lack basic knowledge of budgeting, savings, investing, and debt management are more vulnerable to financial setbacks. By empowering individuals with the tools to understand and manage their finances, we can help them make informed decisions and build long-term financial stability.

Strategy:

Financial Education Programs: Implement community-based financial literacy programs, either through partnerships with local organizations, schools, or mobile platforms. These programs should cover topics like budgeting, saving, credit scores, and investment options.

Example:

Practical Insight:

"MyPath" a nonprofit organization, works with young people in underserved communities to help them build financial literacy and savings skills. They've found that by teaching participants to save and budget, they can reduce financial stress and provide a foundation for building wealth.

Value Created:

These programs reduce fear of financial insecurity by giving people the knowledge to make better decisions, manage resources effectively, and build habits that foster financial resilience.

2. Access to Capital and Credit

Access to capital and credit is one of the largest barriers for underserved communities, particularly those without traditional banking relationships or assets. Without access to loans, savings accounts, or credit, families and small businesses are more likely to fall into poverty cycles.

Strategy:

Microfinance and Alternative Lending Models: Promote microloans, community credit unions, and other alternative lending models that provide small, accessible loans to individuals or businesses without traditional credit histories.

Example:

Practical Insight:

Grameen Bank offers small, low-interest loans to individuals in poverty-stricken areas, particularly women, to help them start small businesses. This model has been successful in many countries, proving that when individuals have access to capital, they can build a path out of poverty.

Value Created:

Providing access to capital enables individuals and small businesses to generate income, create jobs, and reduce the vulnerability of families to sudden financial shocks.

3. Creating Stable Employment and Income Opportunities

Creating stable, sustainable employment opportunities is critical in addressing the root causes of financial insecurity. Many people in underserved communities work in precarious jobs without benefits or long-term stability, exacerbating poverty cycles.

Strategy:

Job Training and Skills Development: Offer job training programs in high-demand sectors such as healthcare, technology, or renewable energy. Tailor programs to the specific needs of underserved communities, and focus on sectors that have room for growth.

Example:

Practical Insight:

Year Up is an organization that provides training, mentorship, and internships to young adults from low-income backgrounds, helping them transition into careers in IT and other fields. By focusing on skills that employers need, they help participants build sustainable careers.

Value Created:

Providing access to skill development programs increases employability, empowers individuals to secure better jobs, and helps them achieve long-term financial stability.

4. Reducing the Fear of Loss Through Social Safety Nets

Many people in low-income communities are driven by a constant fear of losing their jobs, homes, or access to basic services. One of the most effective ways to address these insecurities is by offering social safety nets that provide a cushion against financial setbacks.

Strategy:

Universal Basic Income (UBI) or Conditional Cash Transfers: Implement cash transfer programs or UBI initiatives that provide direct financial support to low-income families. These programs help alleviate the immediate fear of financial loss and offer a stable foundation.

Example:

Practical Insight:

The GiveDirectly Program provides cash transfers to low-income families, allowing recipients to use the funds as they see fit. Research on cash transfers has shown that these initiatives help reduce poverty, improve mental health, and empower families to invest in education, health, and business.

Value Created:

Social safety nets reduce anxiety about loss, enable families to plan for the future, and give them the financial breathing room needed to break out of poverty.

5. Affordable and Accessible Housing Solutions

The fear of losing one's home is a common financial insecurity, and housing instability is a major driver of poverty. High rent costs, eviction threats, and limited access to affordable housing contribute to the cycle of financial insecurity.

Strategy:

Affordable Housing Initiatives: Promote affordable housing projects that offer long-term, stable housing options for low-income families. These initiatives should include not only low-cost housing but also services such as job training, childcare, and healthcare, which address the broader needs of underserved communities.

Example:

Practical Insight:

Habitat for Humanity builds affordable homes and works with families to ensure that they can afford long-term housing. This initiative combines affordable housing with a sense of ownership and community, which can empower families to thrive.

Value Created:

Affordable housing reduces the constant fear of displacement and helps families create stable, long-term living situations. This stability is a critical foundation for financial growth and upward mobility.

6. Leveraging Technology to Improve Access and Reduce Costs

Technology can play a critical role in breaking down the barriers to financial access, education, and healthcare. With the rise of mobile phones and internet access, tech solutions can reach underserved communities and provide them with tools to improve their financial situation.

Strategy:

Mobile Platforms for Financial Inclusion: Create mobile apps that provide financial services like savings, loans, and insurance. Use mobile banking, remittance services, and financial planning tools to help families and individuals in underserved areas.

Example:

Practical Insight:

M-Pesa, a mobile money service, allows users in Kenya and other African countries to send, receive, and store money through their phones. M-Pesa has helped millions of people in low-income communities' access financial services, empowering them to save, manage expenses, and invest in their future.

Value Created:

Technology reduces the cost of financial services and makes them more accessible, enabling underserved populations to save, invest, and access capital in ways that were previously impossible.

7. Promoting Community-Based Solutions and Social Enterprises

Communities themselves often hold the answers to overcoming poverty and financial insecurity. Social enterprises and community-driven initiatives are powerful tools for addressing local challenges while creating value for both individuals and society.

Strategy:

Support for Social Enterprises: Provide grants, training, and resources to local social enterprises that aim to solve specific problems within their communities, such as access to food, healthcare, or employment opportunities.

Example:

Practical Insight:

The Empowerment Program trains and employs people from underserved communities to run local businesses that address community needs. These businesses reinvest profits into further community development.

Value Created:

Social enterprises create jobs, foster community engagement, and address local needs while promoting financial independence and reducing reliance on external aid.

Conclusion:

Tackling the financial insecurities and poverty cycles requires a multi-faceted approach that combines education, access to capital, job creation, social safety nets, housing stability, and technology. By empowering individuals with the knowledge, resources, and opportunities to improve their financial situation, we can help them break free from cycles of poverty. The strategies outlined above provide practical insights that can help create long-term value, address fears of loss and scarcity, and empower underserved communities to achieve greater financial security and independence.

So create products and services that address financial security, such as insurance plans, savings programs, or low-cost essentials. Highlight the fear of scarcity with urgency-based messaging like 'limited time offers' and 'act now to secure your future' to encourage immediate purchase.

The next chapter studies the psychology behind the pursuit of riches and its influence on markets. How aspirational brands and stories inspire individuals to rise above poverty. Practical insights: Creating opportunities that align with people's aspirations.

Chapter 6:

Aspiration for Wealth

– The Poor's Dream of Prosperity

The pursuit of wealth has been a central driver of human behavior for centuries, influencing not only individual lives but also the broader economic landscape. As individuals strive for better living standards and economic freedom, the desire for riches often becomes intertwined with societal values, personal identity, and status. Brands and stories that tap into these aspirations have a unique ability to inspire action, shape market trends, and create new opportunities for growth. Understanding the psychology behind the pursuit of wealth and how it shapes consumer behavior is crucial for businesses looking to empower individuals, especially those from underserved communities, to rise above poverty.

1. The Psychological Drivers Behind the Pursuit of Wealth

The desire for wealth is often rooted in deeper psychological needs. These can include the need for security, self-esteem, status, and personal empowerment. Wealth is seen not just as a means to acquire material goods, but also as a tool to gain respect, freedom, and a sense of accomplishment.

Security and Survival: For many people, especially those living in poverty, the desire for wealth stems from the need for financial security. The fear of scarcity or loss can drive individuals to pursue wealth as a way to escape economic instability and ensure basic needs like housing, food, and healthcare are met.

Self-Actualization: Beyond basic security, wealth is often associated with personal growth, autonomy, and achieving one's potential. Aspirations tied to wealth may reflect a desire to create something meaningful, whether it's a business, a legacy, or an impact on society.

Social Comparison: The influence of social comparison is another powerful motivator. People often look to others—celebrities, successful entrepreneurs, or influencers—whose wealth and success represent the potential rewards of hard work and smart choices. This comparison fosters a desire to emulate those who have achieved financial success.

Status and Identity: Wealth can also represent status, social influence, and recognition. Many individuals pursue wealth as a way to signal their success and differentiate themselves in a competitive social environment.

2. Aspirational Brands: Using the Desire for Wealth to Inspire Action

Aspirational brands are those that tap into the emotional and psychological drivers behind the pursuit of wealth. They market not just a product or service, but an image, a lifestyle, or a vision of what life could look like once their products are in use. These brands appeal to consumers' aspirations by positioning themselves as symbols of success, empowerment, and achievement.

Strategy:

Create Emotional Connections: Successful aspirational brands craft narratives that evoke strong emotions. They don't just sell a product; they sell an idealized vision of life. This could be the dream of financial independence, the status of owning luxury goods, or the empowerment that comes from educational opportunities. By aligning their products with consumers' dreams of wealth and success, these brands inspire individuals to take action.

Example:

Apple has long positioned itself as a brand that represents creativity, innovation, and success. The clean design and high-end technology convey an image of prestige and individuality. Apple doesn't just sell phones and computers; it sells a lifestyle of modernity and achievement.

Practical Insight:

Nike is another great example of an aspirational brand. Through campaigns like "Just Do It," Nike connects its products to the idea of pushing through personal limits and overcoming challenges. For many, buying Nike products is not just about purchasing sportswear; it's about joining a culture of perseverance, success, and achievement.

Value Created:

Aspirational brands make their customers feel that by aligning with their product or service, they are on the path toward personal success. This connection can drive customer loyalty and create a strong emotional bond that encourages long-term spending and advocacy.

3. Stories of Success: How Narratives Drive Aspirations

One of the most powerful tools in inspiring individuals to pursue wealth is the use of stories. Stories -whether through books, movies, or brand marketing- create a narrative that illustrates the journey from struggle to success, highlighting the obstacles overcome and the rewards achieved. These success stories inspire individuals, especially those in underserved communities, to believe that they too can rise above their current circumstances.

Strategy:

Inspire Through Real-Life Successes: Share authentic stories of people who have overcome adversity to achieve success. These stories can resonate deeply with audiences, especially when they see someone who shares their background or challenges succeed.

Example:

Oprah Winfrey's story of rising from poverty to becoming one of the world's richest and most influential women has been a source of inspiration for millions. Her narrative reinforces the idea that, with determination, anyone can achieve success regardless of their background.

Practical Insight:

The "American Dream" narrative has been a staple of advertising and cultural storytelling for generations. It tells the story of individuals who rise from humble beginnings through hard work, innovation, and perseverance. By framing products or services within the context of the American Dream, brands tap into deep psychological drivers and motivate people to take action toward financial success.

Value Created:

Brands that use success stories help consumers see what's possible, creating a sense of hope and motivation. When people see others overcoming obstacles, it can spark the belief that they too can improve their lives and reach their goals.

4. Creating Opportunities That Align with Aspirations

While inspiring individuals through aspirational branding and success stories is crucial, businesses must also create tangible opportunities that align with the aspirations of underserved communities. This means developing products, services, and platforms that not only promise a path to wealth but also provide real avenues for achieving it.

Strategy:

Focus on Access and Empowerment: Companies must offer products or services that provide actual value, not just empty promises. This could include access to education, mentorship, affordable financial services, or platforms that help individuals build their skills and networks.

Example:

Udemy and other online education platforms offer affordable courses that teach people new skills, enabling them to access better job opportunities. These platforms directly address aspirations for career advancement and financial independence by providing affordable and accessible education.

Practical Insight:

Micro-entrepreneurship platforms, such as Etsy or Uber, allow individuals to start businesses with low upfront costs. These platforms empower people to leverage their skills and time to generate income, thus aligning with aspirations for self-sufficiency and wealth-building.

Value Created:

By offering access to tools that enable economic mobility—whether through education, technology, or entrepreneurial opportunities—brands can align with the aspirational desires of individuals in underserved communities.

This creates tangible opportunities that help break the cycle of poverty.

5. The Role of Technology in Democratizing Access to Wealth

Technology plays a pivotal role in creating opportunities that align with the aspirations of individuals, particularly in underserved communities. It enables new business models, enhances access to education, and facilitates global connections that can lead to new wealth-building opportunities.

Strategy:

Leverage Technology to Create Scalable Opportunities: Businesses should build digital platforms that allow underserved populations to access global markets, education, and financial services. This could include everything from micro-lending platforms to e-learning resources to job marketplaces.

Example:

Kiva is a micro-lending platform that connects people who want to help with entrepreneurs in developing countries. The platform democratizes access to capital, enabling individuals in underserved areas to start businesses and generate income.

Practical Insight:

Skill-building apps like Skillshare allow individuals to learn from experts and get access to a community of learners, making it easier for them to upskill and rise above economic challenges.

Value Created:

By democratizing access to technology and resources, businesses provide a scalable way for individuals to build wealth. These platforms create real opportunities that help people act on their aspirations and achieve financial success.

- *Selling Insights*

Develop aspirational products that symbolize upward mobility, such as affordable luxury items, financial education programs, and investment opportunities. Use emotional stories and relatable role models to inspire hope and push consumption.

Conclusion:

The psychology behind the pursuit of riches is deeply tied to human desires for security, self-empowerment, status, and self-actualization. By understanding these psychological drivers, businesses can create products, services, and narratives that align with people's aspirations, particularly in underserved communities. Aspirational brands and success stories serve as powerful motivators, but real value is created when companies provide tangible opportunities that empower individuals to act on their aspirations. By leveraging technology and focusing on empowerment, businesses can help break the cycle of poverty and create lasting pathways to success for those who need it most.

Next chapter explore Balancing moral responsibility with profit-driven motives. Case studies of companies that created wealth ethically by responding to desires.

Chapter 7:

The Ethics of Leveraging Human Desire

Balancing Moral Responsibility with Profit-Driven Motives

In today's business world, the line between ethical responsibility and profit-driven motives can often seem blurred. While companies are fundamentally driven by the need to generate profit, there is growing awareness of the importance of aligning their practices with moral responsibility. Balancing these two aspects—making money while adhering to ethical values—has become an essential strategy for building sustainable, socially responsible businesses. In this chapter, we explore how businesses can achieve this delicate balance and examine case studies of companies that have successfully created wealth ethically by responding to consumer desires.

1. The Tension Between Profit and Ethics

The traditional view of business often emphasizes profit maximization as the primary objective, with ethics playing a secondary role. However, increasing public awareness about social and environmental issues has led to a shift in consumer expectations. People today want to support brands that not only deliver value but also align with their own ethical beliefs and values, especially in areas such as sustainability, labor rights, and community impact.

Strategy:

Companies must integrate ethical principles into their core business models, ensuring that profit-making activities do not come at the expense of social responsibility. This requires companies to not only comply with laws and regulations but to actively consider the broader impact of their operations.

Example:

Patagonia, an outdoor clothing brand, has built its business model around sustainability and environmental advocacy. While its core business is selling high-quality outdoor apparel, the company goes beyond profit-making by engaging in practices that protect the environment, such as using recycled materials, promoting fair labor practices, and even encouraging customers to buy less.

Value Created:

Patagonia has successfully aligned its ethical values with its profit-driven motives. The company's ethical stance has attracted a loyal customer base that values sustainability, while also allowing Patagonia to command a premium price for its products. In fact, the brand's commitment to environmental issues has become one of its most important selling points, driving both profit and social impact.

2. Case Study 1: The Body Shop - Ethical Consumerism and Profit

The Body Shop, a global cosmetics and skincare company, is a prime example of a brand that built wealth while maintaining a commitment to ethical practices. Founded by Anita Roddick in 1976, the company focused on creating high-quality beauty products with an emphasis on natural ingredients, environmental sustainability, and ethical sourcing. The Body Shop also championed issues such as animal rights, fair trade, and community trade.

Ethical Approach:

The Body Shop's business model centered on promoting social causes while still delivering a high-quality consumer product. The company was one of the first to pioneer cruelty-free cosmetics and established community trade partnerships with marginalized producers in developing countries. They also maintained a policy of transparency, clearly communicating their commitment to social issues with their customers.

Profitability:

By tapping into the growing trend of ethical consumerism, The Body Shop attracted a loyal customer base that was willing to pay a premium for products they believed were morally aligned with their values. The company's financial success demonstrated that ethical responsibility could coexist with profit-driven motives.

Value Created:

The Body Shop successfully created a business model that responded to the desires of ethically-minded consumers, balancing moral responsibility with profitability. This not only generated wealth but also sparked a wider movement in the beauty industry toward more ethical, sustainable practices. Eventually, The Body Shop was acquired by L'Oréal, cementing the idea that ethical business models could scale and attract major investment.

3. Case Study 2: Ben & Jerry's - Social Justice and Profit

Ben & Jerry's, the iconic ice cream brand, is another example of a company that has effectively balanced moral responsibility with profit. From its founding in 1978, Ben & Jerry's has been committed to social and environmental causes, including climate change, racial justice, and fair trade.

Ethical Approach:

Ben & Jerry's operates with a "Three-Part Mission" that balances product quality with social impact and economic growth. The company's ingredients are sourced through fair trade partnerships, ensuring that small-scale farmers in developing countries receive fair wages for their work. Additionally, the company has been an outspoken advocate for environmental sustainability, using sustainable packaging and reducing its carbon footprint.

Profitability:

While Ben & Jerry's has a strong ethical foundation, it has also demonstrated how a company can be profitable by aligning with consumer values. The company's bold stances on social justice issues resonate with many of its customers, particularly younger, socially-conscious consumers. Ben & Jerry's brand loyalty has translated into significant sales, especially as consumers increasingly look to support businesses that share their values.

Value Created:

By combining a commitment to social justice with delicious, high-quality ice cream, Ben & Jerry's has built a loyal customer base that is willing to pay a premium for their products. This has allowed the company to continue its advocacy work and grow its business, showing that profitability and social responsibility can be mutually reinforcing.

4. Case Study 3: Toms Shoes - Purpose-Driven Profit

Toms Shoes pioneered the "one-for-one" model, where every pair of shoes sold would result in a donation of a new pair to a person in need. This innovative approach to business combined social impact with profitability, responding to consumers' desire to make a positive difference through their purchasing decisions.

Ethical Approach:

Toms Shoes built its business around the idea that purchasing a product could have a direct and positive social impact. By addressing the global need for footwear in impoverished regions, Toms created a purpose-driven business model that resonated deeply with consumers looking for brands that matched their desire for both quality and purpose.

Profitability:

Toms capitalized on the growing trend of socially-conscious consumerism, turning its "buy one, give one" approach into a major marketing tool. This model allowed Toms to scale rapidly, attract investment, and achieve significant revenue while addressing a key social issue. The model also sparked other businesses to adopt similar giving strategies.

Value Created:

By addressing consumers' desire for both high-quality products and the ability to give back, Toms Shoes created a profitable brand that resonated with ethical consumers. This strategy allowed the company to grow exponentially, with Toms expanding its product offerings and its social mission over time. Even as the company faced challenges in scaling the one-for-one model, it showed that aligning profit with a sense of purpose could build both financial and social capital.

5. Case Study 4: Warby Parker - Affordable Eyewear and Social Responsibility

Warby Parker, a direct-to-consumer eyewear company, disrupted the traditional eyewear market by offering high-quality, stylish glasses at an affordable price. In addition to providing affordable eyewear, the company also created a unique business model focused on social impact.

Ethical Approach:

Warby Parker's "Buy a Pair, Give a Pair" program ensures that for every pair of glasses purchased, another pair is donated to someone in need. The company also focuses on sustainability, using eco-friendly materials in their frames and maintaining transparency in their supply chain.

Profitability:

By offering affordable eyewear while giving back to those in need, Warby Parker tapped into the growing market for socially conscious brands. Their approach has resonated particularly with younger consumers who value both style and social responsibility. The company has successfully built a profitable business while creating a positive impact in the communities it serves.

Value Created:

Warby Parker's combination of affordable pricing, stylish designs, and social responsibility has allowed the company to build a strong brand identity. The company has proven that it is possible to combine profit and ethics in a way that resonates with consumers, resulting in strong customer loyalty and business growth.

- **Selling Insights**

Balance ethical considerations while promoting products. Create campaigns that emphasize sustainable, fair, and transparent practices. Show how consumption can satisfy desires while contributing to the greater good, appealing to socially conscious consumers.

The Path to Ethical Profit

To sum up, these case studies demonstrate that ethical business practices and profit-driven motives can coexist and even reinforce one another. Companies that balance moral responsibility with the pursuit of profit by responding to consumer desires for social impact, sustainability, and fairness can not only drive growth but also create lasting positive change. The key to success lies in integrating ethical values into every aspect of a company's business model, ensuring that profit is generated in a way that benefits not just shareholders, but society as a whole. By doing so, companies can build trust with their customers, foster loyalty, and make a meaningful impact on the world.

Conclusion:

From Understanding to Action

A blueprint for identifying gaps in society's needs and crafting solutions that lead to success and wealth.

As we've explored throughout this book, identifying and addressing the unmet needs in society offers a unique opportunity to create value, drive innovation, and build sustainable wealth. Whether through ethical business practices, fulfilling consumer desires, or crafting opportunities for underserved communities, the pathway from understanding societal gaps to taking meaningful action is both a moral and a strategic endeavor. This conclusion provides a blueprint for transforming insights into impactful solutions, creating businesses that not only generate profit but also address deep, systemic needs.

1. Identify Gaps in Society's Needs

The first step in crafting solutions that lead to both success and wealth is understanding the unmet needs that exist in society. These gaps may be visible in various sectors, such as healthcare, education, housing, or financial services, and often represent areas where traditional solutions have fallen short. Identifying these gaps requires a deep understanding of societal challenges and the willingness to think creatively about how to address them.

Strategy:

Research and Observation: Stay attuned to societal changes, emerging trends, and the evolving needs of different communities. This may involve conducting market research, engaging with community leaders, and listening to the concerns and desires of underserved populations. It also requires empathy—being able to put yourself in the shoes of others to truly understand their struggles.

Practical Insight:

Data and Technology: Use data analytics, social media insights, and advanced technologies like AI to identify trends and patterns that reveal gaps. Technology can help pinpoint inefficiencies, highlight disparities, and discover areas ripe for innovation.

Example:

Mobile Banking in Africa: In many parts of Africa, traditional banking systems have limited reach, leaving large swaths of the population unbanked. The introduction of mobile banking platforms like M-Pesa helped address this gap by offering people access to financial services via their mobile phones, transforming the financial landscape in the region.

2. Craft Solutions That Are Not Only Profitable but Impactful

Once gaps in society's needs are identified, the next step is to create solutions that address these challenges while also aligning with the desire for profit. Crafting such solutions requires a deep understanding of the target market, a commitment to sustainability, and a vision for long-term impact.

Strategy:

Innovative Problem-Solving: Design products, services, or platforms that not only fulfill an immediate need but do so in a way that is scalable, sustainable, and impactful. Focus on how your solution can make a meaningful difference in people's lives, and ensure that this impact is measurable and aligned with your business goals.

Practical Insight:

Human-Centered Design: Implement a design thinking approach—one that focuses on the needs, wants, and limitations of the users. By putting the customer at the heart of the solution, you increase the likelihood of creating a product or service that resonates deeply with your audience and addresses real challenges.

Example:

Tesla and the Electric Vehicle Market: Tesla identified the gap in the electric vehicle market—there was a demand for sustainable, high-performance cars that didn't compromise on design or efficiency. By focusing on innovative technology, environmental impact, and luxury, Tesla created a product that not only served an ecological need but also appealed to consumers' desires for innovation and status, leading to immense success.

3. Scale and Expand Your Reach

Once an initial solution is developed, the next step is to scale and expand its reach. To do this successfully, you must understand how to build a business model that allows for growth while maintaining the core principles that make the solution valuable in the first place. This phase requires strategic partnerships, robust infrastructure, and the ability to pivot when necessary.

Strategy:

Growth with Integrity: Scale your operations while staying true to your core mission. Ensure that as you grow, the quality of your product or service does not diminish, and that your ethical commitments remain at the forefront. Be prepared to face challenges and use them as learning opportunities to improve your offering.

Practical Insight:

Global Expansion: If your solution is effective in one region, explore how it can be adapted and expanded to other areas. Research cultural nuances and market differences to ensure that the solution is relevant and appealing in new locations.

Example:

Airbnb's Global Growth: Airbnb started by solving a local problem—creating affordable and unique travel experiences by renting out spare rooms. Over time, it scaled globally by staying true to its mission of offering personalized, affordable, and unique stays for travelers, while adapting to local needs and regulations.

4. **Align Business with Societal Aspirations**

For a solution to create sustained success and wealth, it must align with both the immediate needs of individuals and the broader societal aspirations. Many of today's consumers, particularly younger generations, increasingly expect brands to take a stand on social and environmental issues. Businesses that understand and embrace this shift will be well-positioned to succeed, as they demonstrate a deeper understanding of their customers' values and aspirations.

Strategy:

Purpose-Driven Business Models: Build your brand and business around a central purpose that resonates with both your target audience and broader societal trends. This could be a commitment to environmental sustainability, social justice, access to education, or health and wellness. Businesses that contribute positively to the world tend to cultivate stronger customer loyalty, trust, and long-term profitability.

Practical Insight:

Transparency and Authenticity: Modern consumers value transparency and authenticity. Ensure that your business practices, sourcing, and operations are aligned with the values you espouse. Show how your business decisions contribute to broader societal goals, and be prepared to provide evidence of your impact.

Example:

Beyond Meat: Beyond Meat capitalized on the growing consumer desire for plant-based food alternatives that align with concerns about health, sustainability, and animal rights. By creating a product that meets these societal aspirations while also providing a profitable business model, Beyond Meat has made a significant impact on both the market and the planet.

5. Measure and Adapt for Long-Term Success

Success and wealth are not just about immediate profits—they are about sustained growth over time. For that, it is essential to measure the impact of your solutions, refine your strategies, and adapt to changing circumstances. Businesses that evolve and respond to feedback can stay ahead of the curve and continue to create value long into the future.

Strategy:

Continuous Innovation and Feedback Loops: Implement systems to regularly assess the effectiveness of your products and services. Gather feedback from customers, stakeholders, and employees to understand what is working and what needs improvement. Use this information to adapt and refine your approach.

Practical Insight:

Data-Driven Decisions: Use data analytics and customer insights to continually refine your offerings. Measure your social, environmental, and financial impacts to ensure that your business is achieving the desired outcomes and providing real value.

Example:

Microsoft's Shift to Cloud Computing: Over the years, Microsoft has shifted its focus from traditional software products to cloud computing. This transition, driven by technological advancements and customer demand for scalable, flexible solutions, helped the company adapt and thrive in an evolving market.

Conclusion: The Path Forward

By identifying gaps in society's needs and crafting solutions that address these challenges, businesses can create value, drive innovation, and build wealth in a way that also benefits society. The key to success lies in understanding what people truly want, creating products and services that meet these needs, and doing so in a way that is sustainable and ethically responsible. By balancing the demands of profit with a commitment to social good, businesses can achieve long-term success and contribute to creating a more equitable and prosperous world.

In the end, wealth is not just measured in financial terms but in the positive impact a business has on the world. The blueprint for achieving both success and wealth involves aligning your business with the greater good, responding to societal needs, and continually innovating to ensure that your solutions remain relevant and effective for the long term.

Table des matières

Introduction: The Nature of Desire 1

Chapter 1: Power and Authority 7

Chapter 2: 20

Beauty and Perception 20

– The Women's Pursuit of Aesthetics 20

Chapter 3: Longevity and Health – The Elderly's Desire for Wellness 37

Chapter 4: 43

Play and Imagination 43

– The Children's World of Games 43

Chapter 5: 57

Fear of Scarcity 57

– Overcoming Poverty through Security 57

Chapter 6: 74

Aspiration for Wealth 74

– The Poor's Dream of Prosperity 74

Chapter 7:..90
The Ethics of Leveraging Human Desire.......90
   - Selling Insights..103
Conclusion: 105
From Understanding to Action 105

www.ingramcontent.com/pod-product-compliance
Lightning Source LLC
Chambersburg PA
CBHW071035240526
45469CB00006BD/2220